BEADWEAVING
Make Jewelry & Accessories with Beads

By

Joann Rohrbach

Contents

The World of Beads

Welcome to the world of making beautiful, handcrafted jewelry and accessories with beads. Beaded jewelry is a great way to get involved in a fun hobby and maybe even a home business. Many beginners sometimes have to do a lot of research to find practical information needed about beads and beading. This handy guide will help you get started toward that goal without all the extra legwork. It will be your beading companion.

If you already know about beading, this guide will help you be a better beader. It offers many helpful tips and ideas that you may not have seen before.

People start beading for many different reasons. Some like working with their hands and do it as a fun hobby. Others do it to make extra cash by selling their handcrafted jewelry or just for the fun of giving a handmade gift. The addiction knows no boundaries. Beaders have been showing up everywhere and you could easily become a beadaholic.

Wait a minute, you say, beading? Wasn't that what back-to-nature folks did during the 1960's? The idea may be old-fashioned, but today's modern beaders are happily stringing them along. We can now find better quality beads, more selections to pick from and more places to find them. People, like you, are walking into local craft or bead shops, and asking for advice. You only need start small, beginning with a minor Investment to get started. Whether a beader will save money depends on his or her taste. You can purchase a deluxe bead stringing kit, which usually includes several types of needle nose pliers, tweezers, scissors, and wire cutters. However, these things are not always necessary. Also, the smaller beads can be purchased for much less while larger heads and stones used in jewelry are sold by the piece.

Making beaded jewelry may remind you of crocheting. The first row is worked, and then subsequent rows are worked into the first row in a predictable way. It is an inexpensive way to make beautiful pieces that would cost you a lot more to buy them already made. It's even possible to make jewelry pieces that look like the ones that cost a fortune. There's a beautiful necklace in the Smithsonian that sells for around $400. Jewelry pieces like this may be original, but you can make your own originals for a lot less.

Whatever your goals are, shop around. It's fun to browse and it helps plant idea seeds in your imagination. Sometimes we can come up with the best ideas by seeing what someone else has made with beads. Try visiting some shops near you. Don't be afraid to ask questions. Some craft and hobby shops hold classes that teach how to make jewelry. Most are more than willing to answer your questions.

There are so many things you can do with beads. Once you learn the basic beading procedures, you can vary your designs by using the many different styles, sizes and colors of beads that are available to you. Whether you want to use your imagination and design your own jewelry or just follow a simple pattern, you'll have fun. You will see that the finished pieces you've made will give you a sense of pride. In fact, when your friends and family see the beautiful pieces you have created; they'll be impressed and want some too.

You can make earrings, necklaces, bracelets and rings to match any outfit for any occasion. Or you can make your lovely jewelry and accessories to sell and make a few extra dollars. Either way, you'll be glad you learned the art of beadweaving. The main problem in getting started making jewelry is fear of the unknown. Once the mystery is gone, so is the fear as you will see when you become an experienced beader.

Above all, please try to be patient with yourself. The first pair of earrings most people make usually don't turn out perfect. But when you make things with beads, you can tear them out and start over again if you're not satisfied with the finished look of your jewelry piece. Nothing is wasted but some thread and a little bit of time. Just like anything else, you'll get better and faster as you go along. The more you make and practice your new hobby, the better your jewelry will be.

Remember, making beautiful, handcrafted jewelry is wonderful. Part of the fun is having a good time while doing it.

Make Jewelry and Accessories with Beads

Who would think that handmade crafts would play such an important part in our lives? Everywhere we look, we see touches of Grandma's crochet or Grandpa's woodworking pieces in our lives.

We all have a creative work within us waiting to get out. We just need to tap that spark and find out what wonderful sort of artwork we can produce with our own two hands.

I'm not talking about the sort of cute, little pieces of this and that which come off an assembly line. I'm referring to those special pieces that are produced with our own two hands through our loving supply of time, patience and persistence.

Even when our children bring home their special artwork from school, they touch our hearts. The drawings and special pieces they make with the help of their teacher's directions are crafts.

That's the beginning of our creative and crafting process and starts from the time we are born one way or another. Even an auto mechanic has a certain knack when he crafts and keeps that car running.

I remember well when I was a little girl; my father's hand-loomed carpets were something everyone wanted to own. His yule logs decorated with pine cones and candles graced our table at Christmas for many years. This is the sort of thing that memories are made of

7

when you place sentimental value on your handiwork.

Today, talented craftsmen stay busy when they can fill a need for so many beautiful items and also make money while they're at it. Hand crafted items are more in demand than ever and crafts can be a way to have an enjoyable hobby, make a little extra money selling your handiwork, or it can be the start of a booming business.

Crafts are old-fashioned and still in style! Crafts are a growing industry today. Crafts are big business. Why crafts? Have you looked around lately? Handmade goods are everywhere.

From beautiful crocheted items to wooden knick-knacks, handicrafts come in various colors and sizes enough to suit everyone. People everywhere buy handcrafted and homemade treasures because they are unique and special. Hopefully, most people will treasure and enjoy them for years. Who would think those treasures we make with our own two hands would be worth a few bucks.

I'm glad I'm a craftaholic! There are so many crafty things we can make if we use our imaginations. Maybe you're already a crafter. If not, give it try. But beware! You can turn into a craftaholic too.

You can buy handcrafted items everywhere these days that have many different offerings in colors, types, sizes, and prices. Some handicrafts can cost very little. Others can be very expensive. We could spend hours browsing before we make a decision on the perfect item for ourselves. Then we see it across the room. Our eyes glow and our hearts pound. There it is, the perfect little what-not for our corner shelf. This is what sometimes happens when people and our handicrafts come together. Its great knowing we are responsible for making many people happy.

You can buy supplies everywhere these days. You'll find a good selection at department stores as well as specialty shops. There's many craft stores cropping up all over and carry just about everything we need to make a particular project. You can also buy online and many places offer free patterns.

If you're not sure how to make something you really like, you might try starting out with a kit if it's available. At least that way, we have a pattern and a starting point if we're not sure where to begin. Purchasing a kit is a good way to learn. Afterwards, you might feel brave enough to buy the supplies you need and make your own designs like I did. You can make designs for just about anything if you are really interested in how it's all put together.

If you love crafts too, you can make lovely things for yourself. You can make dozens or just a few. You can keep them all for yourself, or give some away as gifts. You can also sell your finished handcrafted pieces and easily make a few bucks.

You can be your own boss and make your own hours. You can enjoy working at something you love instead of just going to a boring job, or make a little extra money besides your regular job. You can skip the long and tedious commutes to work. You can take a holiday when you feel like it. You can save money on clothes and dress as you wish. You can turn your nose up at on-the-job politics.

Does all the above sound appealing to you? Then join the growing number of artists, crafters, hobbyists and collectors who are turning their interests into profits. You can work out of your own home making and selling your handicrafts too.

You can sell them at stores that take craft items on consignment, especially specialty shops that carry gift items. You can sell them at craft shows and flea markets. They're great fund raisers too.

I love making things just for the pleasure of it. I adore everything about handcrafted items. I can appreciate that each is different and beautiful in its own way. It's also nice to know we can make a buck by making something lovely with our own two hands and selling it.

I just keep crafting along. Once you try it, you might decide to do the same. Remember to have fun as you work.

Why beads? Have you looked around lately? Beads are everywhere. They're strung on shoe laces and hanging from key chains. You'll find them adorning clothing and hair. Not to mention all those accessories we carry around with us every day, such as backpacks, pocketbooks and yes, they're even on eyeglasses.

Beads are basic, popular, and always in style. Who would think those little treasures would be worth a few bucks?

I'm glad I'm a beadaholic! Of all the crafts we can make, beads are so versatile. They're as tiny as bird seed and large as eggs. They're fancy and vibrant as a rainbow or plain and cool as sand.

They were onto something in the sixties with the peace movement and bead revival but nothing like the bead craze of today. I guess we're not exactly New Age hippies but New Century ones instead.

I love making things with beads just for the pleasure of it. I love everything about them! I can appreciate that each one is different in all its beauty and glory. It's nice to know we can make a buck by making something lovely with our own two hands and selling it. In the meantime, I plan to just keep stringing them along.

History of Beads

Glass beads have been made for about 9,000 years. They come in all shapes, colors, finishes, and appearances. For most of their history, glass beads were more than a craft, and more than an art. They were equivalent to money, and were traded.

The art of bead design was originally brought to the United States from France. It had its day in the mid-Victorian era, when beads were used extensively on clothing and in home furnishings. All the women's magazines of the day carried instructions for fancy beadwork. The most popular were beaded flowers made of glass beads strung on fine wire. Then when fashions changed, bead design kind of vanished for a number of years.

The first bead societies were formed from Los Angeles and San Francisco in the United States, to foreign cities such as London, England and Munich, Germany. Such bead treasures can be found across the world. Venetian trade beads come from West Africa. Silver beads come from Bali, crystal beads from Austria and clay beads are found in Peru.

Because glass is older than written history, the origin of the glass bead can only be traced through archaeology. The first known glass beads were made by melting together silica, a major component of all sand, with certain other ingredients, such as soda and lime, as the soda hastens the melting of silica and the lime hardens the finished product.

The earliest known beads are believed to have been made about 12,000 BC. They were found in Egypt, but were most likely brought there from Asia. They were made of stone and covered with a green glaze. Their green color was the natural result of using crude sand and crude soda. The first hints of transparency appeared in translucent blue beads dated about 1570 BC.

A molded glass bead was found at the site of the Queen's tomb. Queen Ra-Ma-Ka was the first queen of the Egyptian Empire, who lived about 1447 BC. Thousands of beads molded in the shape of flowers and fruits were produced around 1200 BC, and small white cylinder beads were produced by the millions and used to decorate the wrapping of mummies.

Other lands throughout the Mediterranean area were producing beads by 1300 BC. A new empire finally destroyed Egypt's importance in glass bead making. In 30 BC, the Roman emperor added Egypt to his list of conquests and demanded tribute in glass. His demands kept the Egyptian foundries busy for forty years until the fires began to die about AD 14.

It was about this time that the Roman emperor ordered skilled glass workers from Egypt and Syria to migrate to Rome and establish a glass industry there. Glass making became a major industry and beads became relatively unimportant among the many new products being produced.

Since first introduced by Columbus in 1492, glass trade beads and beaded articles have held a fascination for many Americans.   Until the mid-1960's, the vast majority of beadwork was made by a few Native Americans who had generations of traditions to rely upon for inspiration and instruction. While it is still true that most beadwork on sale is still Indian-made, many Americans and Europeans have become interested in the art form.

Working at Home

Let's get started in our new beading adventures and these simple steps will tell you how.

First, you will need a place to work. Your kitchen table is fine. A desk in the corner of a quiet room will work. You will need good lighting. Natural daylight is always best. Otherwise, you may want to use an overhead light or a small lamp near your work area. A flexible lamp with a swing arm that can be moved where the light is needed most is nice. You can also purchase magnifying lamps that sometimes make it easier to see those tiny beads and jewelry pieces. Do what is most comfortable for you.

Beading takes some concentration. Many people can work with background music or the TV playing. You might enjoy a little music while you work. Others need total quiet.

Your home office can be the kitchen table or an entire room devoted to your work. No matter how large or small your space, it should be comfortable as well as efficient.

Are you a crafty person? Do you love making things with your own two hands? Whether you make handicrafts as a fun hobby or to sell and make a profit from them, you can never be too organized.

You can work anywhere, even at your kitchen table. I've done that many times, but have always kept a little corner to store my supplies. No matter what type of crafting you do, it helps a great deal to have our supplies and tools handy and available for when we need them.

You might want to set aside some closet space, a book-shelf, a big storage box under your bed or perhaps you have a kitchen cupboard you can use for this purpose.

I have a bookshelf that holds all my crafting books and patterns. I love to crochet as a hobby and have my yarn, crochet needles, etc. stored in a cabinet in my spare bedroom along with my beading supplies. I often take my crochet work and snuggle in a comfortable chair, crocheting away as I watch a movie on TV.

Not everyone has a spare room at their disposal. In times past, when I didn't have the space, I used storage crates that look like milk crates and stocked them one on top of another in one of the closets. I still use those to this day to store things in. Being a pack-rat and saving things "I might need one day", the crates have been more than useful to me.

One of my friends keeps her needlepoint work in one of those large vinyl bags with handles that she got from a book club. She carries it with her wherever she goes. How's that for convenient? When she's not using it, she stores it on a corner shelf in her laundry room.

I have my computer equipment set up in the spare bedroom along with one of those handy folding tables that I use to make jewelry. That way, I can work when I want and everything I need is at my fingertips.

I design and make lovely jewelry and accessories, mostly with beads. I have a table setup for this purpose. It's one of those folding tables many people use for camping. It's long and when I spread out my thread and supplies, I have more than ample space to work. Beading takes concentration and it's not easily done in the midst of a high traffic or a noisy area of the house.

I have tons of beads and other jewelry findings that I keep nearby on a small bookshelf. That way, when I need something, all I must do is grab the right container. I store my beads and findings in sandwich bags, then place them in those plastic containers with dividers. It's easy to see at a glance, everything in the container that way.

My table holds a good magnifying lamp. Sometimes, this is very useful for seeing and working with tiny objects. I have a tray containing my tools, needle nosed pliers, scissors of various sizes, craft glue, etc.

Having my own little corner has helped tremendously and it will help you too. Everything is at my fingertips when I sit down to work.

If you don't have a little corner of your own, then make one. There's got to be a place that you can stash your tools and supplies until you need them.

Clean out a closet to store your work tools and equipment. You can also add shelves if your work area allows. Wheeled storage bins are a great idea. They allow you to move your tools easily. Organizers are another option for storage. Those affordable plastic containers come in all shapes and sizes. They are good for storage and you can stick them under your bed or stack them in a corner.

You'll find after a while that it saves time and energy when they are at your fingertips. If you have a quiet corner in a room you can make yours to sit and work, that would be great.

You might find too, that your creative juices will flow better because you'll feel special having your own little space. Before you know, your lovely handicrafts will be on display for all to admire.

Here are some things to consider when setting up your work space:

Do you like bright sunlight streaming in or do you prefer dim lighting?

Do you like being near a window or do they distract you?

Do you like working alone or being near other people?

Is there enough space for a desk, table, or other work tools?

Naturally, if you are a night person, then you will want to work quietly without disturbing the rest of the household that may be sleeping.

Crafts can be a fun and profitable business for anyone who has the determination to do it. It's an especially good business for retirees, couples who want to work as a team, and stay at home parents. It's also a good venture as a partnership when a husband, wife, family members, or frineds enjoy the challenge of working together. You can turn your handiwork into a full-time or part-time venture, depending on your lifestyle.

The craft business can be flexible and fit any schedule if you make time for it. The biggest requirement is self-discipline with a little enthusiasm thrown in for good measure. Many crafts do not require artistic skills nor do you have to be a creative genius. There are many good books and classes available to help you learn a craft of your choice. If you have a hobby and already make a craft that you love, then you're way ahead of the game. If you are passionate about making something special with your own two hands, then your enthusiasm will pay off in the long run. The end results will be profits as well as pride in yourself and your handicraft.

Making crafts is a mix of lifestyle and culture. Making crafts for oneself is a fulfilling hobby, one that pleases and makes us happy. Selling crafts is a business. To be a successful craftsman, you must integrate them both. Crafts as a hobby and a business give us that human touch. They connect and bring us together. They help us stay in touch with others. Again, have you ever felt that connection when you stood in line to make a purchase at a department store? It's not quite the same feeling as knowing your treasured item was hand-crafted instead of mass-produced and hot off an assembly line.

We live in a very complex society. But yet, with all the modern technology at our fingertips, we have more and better options than any other time in history. We can buy, sell, consume, advertise and research at the push of a button. The World Wide Web has made everything possible and big dreams are yet to be made, especially in the craft field.

If you think crafts could be an option as a home-based business for you, then you've only just begun on a fun and exciting journey. It could be a venture that will hopefully take you where you want to go.

This book won't offer get-rich-quick-schemes. But if you can create quality handicrafts, you can likely turn them into a business that makes profits from all your hard work.

I've been interested in crafts for many years. I've been on both ends of making and buying hand-crafted treasures. I've labored with love and happily played as I dabbled in my favorite craft. For me, designing and making lovely jewelry and accessories (mostly with beads) became an all-consuming profession. As I became more adept at finding what I needed to design and make my jewelry, I realized the profit potential that existed. I simply devoured any information about my hobby and before I knew it, became very knowledgeable in many areas. I know just where to buy supplies, how to put it all together and where to sell my finished goods. With a little research and the motivation to learn, you can do it too.

Most important, enjoy what you do. Start making a list of what you think you might need to get started.

There are opportunities to make money working at home, making jewelry. You can sell your work on your own by selling at flea markets and placing things on consignment. There are some companies that will pay you to make their jewelry at home.

Most of these companies pay you for assembling jewelry to their specifications. They usually buy the earrings in units of 25 or 50 pieces (or pairs) of all one style and/or color. Either way, you are considered self-employed and are responsible for buying your own materials and paying your own taxes.

This type of home work, which is called the cottage industry, is catching on across the country and becoming more and more popular. The good side is that you can be your own boss and set your own hours. You can be in complete control of your financial goals. You save time and costly travel expenses. You don't have to go out in bad weather. You won't have to worry about finding a babysitter if you have children. You can work while they are asleep or in school.

The bad side is that it does not always provide a weekly

paycheck, unless you can produce on a regular basis. Also, you do not get benefits or paid holidays.

It takes work and dedication to work at home. You must learn to say no more often to interruptions and discipline yourself to work at least a few hours a week.

Many companies offer home employment and will train you because it saves them money. They don't have to provide a workplace. They also save by not having to pay benefits, insurance, social security or other taxes. This allows them to be more competitive and to sell their products at a lower price.

You must research home assembly on the Internet. There are many directories that you can buy that will give you a list of these companies and you can choose one or several that interests you most.

Most of these companies do require you to purchase their non-refundable starter kit which is a very small investment for a chance to make money at home. This allows you the opportunity to see if you can make their jewelry. They do this because although many people would like to work at home, not everyone follows through and finishes what they start.

Therefore, most companies simply couldn't afford to give away the starter kits. When you purchase their starter kit, they will set you up as a home assembler. This shows them that you are serious about working at home. Sometimes they will send you a free sample or one may be purchased for a nominal fee so that you can see what the finished product looks like.

You will also be responsible for buying your own materials, and some of the companies will reimburse you for this. Most of the companies also sell the jewelry supplies needed to make the jewelry. But as you become more experienced, you may decide that you can save money by purchasing the supplies elsewhere.

Do a search on the Internet for work at home directories and you will see many listings of this kind. Write a brief letter to the company of your choice asking for information about assembling their jewelry. Most of them will require a long, business size stamped, self-addressed envelope (SASE) for this purpose. When they send you the information, you can decide at that time if it is agreeable to you. Keep track of the date, names and addresses of the companies you write to and mark them off your list when the replies come back so you don't forget anything or contact them twice by mistake.

Craft fairs sometimes seem like a direct link to consumers with no middle man involved. If you make and sell handcrafted goods, you might want to consider them as a selling outlet. Crafts fairs run the gamut of sizes from small-town events to those that serve as celebration to expansive affairs in major cities. Many people work at making their handicrafts all year long, and then attend craft fairs to sell them.

We can all relate to past days when we've seen peddlers, tinkers, hucksters and gypsies trading or selling their goods for other services or hard cash. We've also seen the many large towns having open-air markets where craftspeople and peddlers could hawk their wares. Most of us have looked around at malls across the country where crafters sold their handicrafts to mall shoppers. Many of them have kiosks set up in the middle of the mall. There are also many craft malls, where there's nothing but craft shops linked together.

It's likely that craftspeople must travel from craft fairs to craft fairs selling their goods. Unless your town is a central point for a crafts marketplace, one must do some traveling to keep up with the craft fair circuit. But you don't necessarily have to travel. If you keep your eyes open, you will find plenty of craft fairs in your town to keep you busy and with a decent cash flow available.

Some craft fairs held in major cities are big deals. Crafters who promote certain items go all out and if you "belong" with your handicraft, you're in. You must be organized and plan carefully. The more crafts fairs you attend, the more important scheduling becomes. Application deadlines must be met, booth fees or deposits paid and travel arrangements made.

Craft fairs are easy to get into and offer a great opportunity to present your work to possible buyers. You have a direct link with consumers and craft wholesalers. Some are looking for certain items in particular that interests them. Others are looking for anything and everything. Out of curiosity, they don't know what they want until they see it. We can't underestimate the power of impulse buying. But many come just to browse and have a good time, not to buy anything. More often than not, they will see something they like and buy it anyhow.

It can be a challenge at best having enough stock to meet the demand and having the time to replenish your stock. It's also tedious and time-consuming setting up and maintaining your booth or space.

Craft fairs are a way for you to sell your handicrafts. Watch your newspaper listings where you will hopefully find more than enough of them to keep you busy. If you belong to craft clubs, they sometimes sponsor them. Look in your yellow pages to see if there are some quarterly, semi-annual or annual fairs that are held in your area.

The main drawback that I've found in selling at craft fairs is that it's like constantly job hunting. Looking for work can wear us down so much to where we get burnout. After a while, we won't be productive because we're tired. Although crafts fairs can be a good way to sell handicrafts occasionally, I wouldn't want to live and breathe it as an ongoing process. Yet at the same time, many crafters love the challenge.

We all have choices and know what's best for us. Try it, you just might like it. While you're at it, check your local craft and hobby stores for more information and craft fairs scheduling. Here are some helpful tips:

1. Research the company you are interested in as much as you can. Make sure you understand their terms and

what they expect from you. Try to obtain a picture or sample of their finished products. Sometimes the items you will be making are easier or more difficult than you think. If you have questions, ask before you get involved or spend any money.

2. Call or write the Better Business Bureau to make sure the company has no complaints filed against them. The time or cost of a stamp or a phone call is well worth it. Remember, it's always better to be safe than sorry.

3. Keep records of your earnings. If you make over a certain amount of money in one year, you will be required to pay taxes on it. You can obtain a copy of the 1040 SE (Self-Employment Tax Form) from the IRS. If possible, make a copy of checks paid to you for your files before you cash it.

4. Keep all your receipts. You can deduct your expenses on your taxes by using the 1040 C (Profit or Loss from Business form). Also, you can call or write the IRS for their free booklet, Publication 334 - Tax Guide for Small Business. It explains what you can deduct such as: part of your home used for business, a percentage of your utility bills, postage and shipping costs, supplies and materials used for manufacturing your jewelry, etc. The good thing is that you only pay taxes on the profit you have made after you take all your deductions which may only be a small amount the first year. Above all, be sure to pay yourself. You can deduct your pay as an expense.

5. Call around to see what shipping and postage costs are. Some companies will reimburse you all or part of the shipping costs. You may want to purchase insurance in case your work is lost. You think it won't happen to you, but it's a lot of your time and labor lost if it does. Call USPS and UPS for charts that give you the rates you need. UPS will come to your home and pick up your packages for an additional charge, no matter how many packages you ship. They also include insurance for the first hundred dollars that the package is worth. You need to pay extra to get insurance for regular mail. The 3-Day Priority mailer from the post office is also a quick way to get the package there quickly. Then again, it all depends on the shipping specifications of the company.

Time Management

If you work at home doing crafts, writing or anything else, your time is your most valuable asset. Time is on your side if you manage it well. Self-discipline and motivation are often the biggest problems and you must learn to say no to those time wasters. It's your time and you may use it any way you want. But in order to succeed in any work at home project or business, you must set your own pace in order to get your work done.

Naturally, we all have things aside from our homework that we must do. We have appointments to make, social obligations to meet, housekeeping to maintain and spending quality time with friends and family who are important to us. It's not easy, but if we manage our time properly, we can work around many things.

You might take advantage of the time your children are in school. If you work days and can only make time in the evenings or on weekends, try to plan small blocks of time around this. I often do that myself. It's surprising how much I can get done before I go grocery shopping, after I've cooked dinner and so forth. Those little blocks of time add up to big chunks that will help you succeed.

You might make a list and do priority things first as they come up. If you have a sick pet on your hands, your first priority is getting him to the vet. Some things come up that we don't expect and we have no choice but to work around them.

I have a routine and it helps get me through my day. The first things I do in the early morning are read and answer my mail. I find a routine helps me stay organized.

I often start a project the night before that I'll finish the following day. If I have nothing started that way, I'll look through my notes to see what I want to work on next and line up my materials. That way, in between working on several things, meeting appointments and so forth, I have a starting point to add to in one of those blocks of time.

Crafting should be fun as well as productive. Don't demand too much of yourself and only do what you're capable of. If you don't finish up a project today, it will be waiting for you tomorrow. If you push yourself too much, you'll become depressed, tired and stressed out. It's difficult to work when we're feeling down that way.

All of us are tempted to take time off and that's okay too. But we can't afford to succumb to those feelings too often or else we miss important deadlines and other commitments. We have a reputation to uphold too.

Just do the best you can and let others know that you are busy. Many people think because we work out of our home, we're not really working. That's probably our biggest drawback. Above all, don't feel guilty about saying no to time wasters.

Make a plan and stick to it. As you get through each day, even if you only accomplish a few things on your list, you'll feel proud of yourself. You will feel somewhat happy and secure in knowing that tomorrow might be even better.

Remember it's your life and your time. Do with it what you want before the time flies and it's gone forever. Smile and be a happy beader!

Making Beading Easier

The materials listed below will help make the assembly of your jewelry easier, but they are not necessary.

Thimble -You may prefer to use a thimble when beading. However, it might be difficult and awkward to use one with tiny beads.

Needle threader - Beware when you use these. With beginner's persistence, you may break the needles because the hole in the needle is so small, the threader does not pull the thread through too easily. You can break many needles before you realize this. They don't work for me and I don't use them even though they sometimes come with the needles. However, you can use them with larger needles.

Beeswax - Run your thread over the beeswax before you begin. It will help keep your thread from splitting. It also makes threading your needle easier. You can also use soap or candle wax.

Working surface cloth - When working with beads, a soft surface is best. Use a solid color so that you can see the beads well. White works best for me. You can use a place mat or any other soft cloth such as a folded sheet or pillow case.

Flat bead containers - You can use small, flat containers for individual colors. Plastic craft organizers are nice because they have several compartments. Some people like to string their beads right out of the containers (like those plastic sandwich holders with lids). You can also keep the beads in separate plastic, folding sandwich bags, one for each type and color bead. I place my beads by size and color in an ordinary sandwich bag and then place each bag in the organizer compartment. That way, I can pour what I need onto my work surface.

Beads must be culled because they should be as uniform in size as possible. If you come across an oddball as you bead, discard it. Or if it's easier, pick out the oddball beads that stand out before you start. You will want each piece of jewelry to look as uniform as possible.

You can use graph paper to make your own designs. You may want to make a copy of the paper and keep one as your original in case you want to try designing lots of jewelry pieces. This way, you won't run out of graph paper. You can also purchase design software for beads that enables you to view how different color combinations look.

Remember, when you are designing your jewelry. If you want to make the earrings smaller, use fewer beads across the bead base and fewer beads for the length. Also shorten the dangles or fringes by using fewer beads. You can use variations in colors of beads and make shapes in the middle of your earrings or other jewelry piece such as a red heart, or a yellow sun, etc. Mix and match colors sometimes look interesting when the colors harmonize.

About Ear Wires - You may use any type of ear wires you prefer for your earrings. Kidney shaped ear wires are very simple to use. You may prefer French hooks (sometimes called Fish hooks) for very long earrings so that they hang nicely on the ear. Clip-ons and posts can be used too. All the above come in non-allergenic, different colors, surgical steel, gold, silver, brass, etc. These can be attached by sewing them in or slipping them on after your earrings are finished. Gently open the ring with tweezers or needle nose pliers, slip it through the top center of the earring and close.

The Thread & Knots - As you pass through the bead with the needle and thread, the needle should be in a slanted position touching the inside of the bead. If you are not careful and try to pass through the thread itself, your needle will snag and split the thread. Pull the beads close on the thread, but not too tight or your work will look bunchy and kinky. Your work should lay flat with no thread showing, but not too loose either.

The knots are always hidden by pulling the thread back down through the bead after you make your knot. Then, gently pull the knot dawn into the bead, you can feel and hear it make a light popping noise. This way your work looks neat and no knots will be showing.

After pulling the knot down into the bead, a dab of clear nail polish or non-water base glue will insure the knot from coming untied, but this is entirely up to you depending on the tightness of your finished knots. I don't use it myself but many people do.

Belding Cortlcelli's Nymo (nylon) brand thread, size 0, 00 or A is best for the smaller beads. Size D is medium thread and size F is heavy enough to handle larger stringing projects. Heavier thread or stretch elastic can be used for rings, necklaces and bracelets. But the thread, like the needle, must sometimes go through the beads several times in the earrings, so it must be very fine. Mono filament (like fishing line) will not work well with this type of bead design. The thread usually comes in white, black or beige. I've seen a rainbow of colors available. You will probably use white most often, unless you prefer using another color. Cotton wrapped polyester thread that is waxed will work for beading, but it is not as strong and may not hold up as long as the Nymo will.

Here are some materials needed to make basic jewelry pieces.

Scissors - A pair of small, sharp, embroidery scissors with long points for cutting threads close to the beads.

Thread - Use very fine thread (size O or 00) for projects that the thread must go through the beads several times, such as in some styles of earrings. Nymo (nylon) thread is very strong.

Beading Needles - Size 10, 11, 12 or 13. The bigger the size used, the smaller the needle. Size 10 is larger than size 13. A very fine, narrow needle is used for beading because sometimes it is necessary to go through the beads several times. It's a good idea to have an extra needle on hand in case you break one.

Bugle Beads - Use any color and length. Sizes 3/16", 1/4" and 1/2" will look good with the tiny seed beads. Also try to mix and match sizes just to see the different looks that can be created, as long as they fit together well.

Seed Beads - Use any color, size 10 or 11. The bigger the size used, the smaller the bead. For example, size 11 is a smaller bead than size 10. These sizes are very easy to find.

Ear Wires - Use any type you prefer as long as they have a loop or hole in them so that you can attach them to your earrings.

Other - Use other types of beads, clasps or jewelry findings needed to complete your jewelry pieces. You might add a charm or other decorations to your piece.

Remembering where you purchased your jewelry supplies or what projects you used them for may be helpful to you later on. It will save you time if you need or want to buy more of the same. If you don't have a good memory, keep the information about the supplies you purchase by saving the cardboard or paper that comes on the bags. Write down the type, color, size and style number so that if you want to use them again, you will be able to get the right ones. This applies to beads, ear wires, etc. I do this so when I need to reference something, I can find it quickly.

Now you've got all the basics to get started.

Beads – All About Them

All beads are not created equal. Glass beads are blown and excreted on a rod, cut and polished. They are close, but not uniform in size. The best beads in the world come from Czechoslovakia. Some come from Taiwan and China. The larger the bead size, the smaller the bead. For example, #15 seed bead is tiny as compared to #10. Much larger still would be #6.

Here are some descriptions of various bead styles to help you become familiar with them.

Hank - Bunch of beads strung with 10 to 14 strands. You can buy a smaller quantity of beads in bags.

Bugle Beads - Tubular shaped beads in sizes 2MM to 30MM. The most popular sizes used are: 3/16", 3/8", 1/4", 1/2", or 1" in length. They are available in all the colors and styles of seed beads: iris, silver lined, transparent, opaque, etc.

Seed Beads - are tiny beads. One of the most popular sizes used and found easily are size 10 and 11. You can find glass beads or acrylic (plastic) ones. Glass seed beads are more desirable and look more beautiful when used in a jewelry piece. The acrylic ones may be better if you are making jewelry for a child. They also make nice ornaments for the Christmas tree.

Delica Beads (Delicas) - are very tiny sliced tubes, and are somewhat like working with blocks, instead of round balls. They are widely used in the making of amulet purses. Most people select delicas by code numbers to go with project patterns. Some of these beads are fairly expensive; they are very high quality, very regular in size and are very popular. Instead of being rounded like most beads, they are shaped like a cylinder with very large holes, and give a tile-like appearance to the finished beadwork.

About Weights and Measures - Use the following information for future reference. It will become second nature to you after a while. For now, all you need to make a pair of earrings is 1 small bag each of bugle beads and seed heads.

A hank is about 10 to 14 strands of beads strung together. How many beads you get depends on the size of the bead. Below are some examples:

#10 seed beads, approx. 3,300 beads per hank.

#11 seed beads, about. 2.2mm, about 4,500 beads per hank.

#8 delicas are about 3.3mm and mostly come in tubes.

#8 seed beads are about 3mm

#2 (3/16") bugle beads, about 1,200 beads per hank.

#3 (1/4") bugle beads, about 900 beads per hank.

The larger beads are usually sold in bags or packages. For example: #5 & #6 large seed heads (or pony beads) contain approx. 350 beads per package. #5 (1/4") bugle beads contain approx. 300 beads per package, depending on the weight.

A large 100 gram bag of bugle or seed beads is pretty close to 3 1/2 oz. and equals approx. 2 1/2 hanks. Smaller bags of bugle or seed beads at 20 grams or even 8 grams can be purchased.

Bead Types - There are many types of shiny glass beads that are considered fancy beads. Following are a few examples:

Opaque beads are a solid color bead with a dull finish. They are somewhat matte in appearance and are very effective when used in Native American designs.

Ceylon beads have a milky luminescent surface and appear to have a pearl-like finish.

Transparent (some light passes through the bead) . Transparent Silver Lined (light passes through the bead, bead hole is silver lined).

Transparent Luster (pearl like finish, more subtle look than transparent silver lined).

Transparent Rainbow (Aurora Borealis rainbow finish, often multiple colors).

OP = Opaque (no light passes through the bead).

OPL = Opaque Luster (has a pearl-like luster finish).

OPR = Opaque Rainbow (opaque with an Aurora Borealis finish, often in multiple colors).

M = Metallic (has a metallic look).

MR = Metallic Rainbow (multiple color metallic).

C = Ceylon (pearl-like finish, similar to Opaque Luster, but more subdued and the colors are often softer).

MA = Matte (Frosted appearance, very popular, Opaque unless indicated otherwise, sometimes 2 or 3 tone).

S-MA = Semi-Matte (not as shiny as most beads, but not quite a matte finish either.

V = Velvet Matte with a very soft, velvety look and feel).

Iris is opaque with a metallic look and has an iridescent finish on the surface. They are widely used because of their rich look and design versatility.

Rainbow beads are similar to iris, but are transparent. They are lighter colors and appear crystalline.

Silver-lined are transparent beads of any color with the hole lined in silver. The center holes are sometimes square instead of round and may be easier to weave. They appear to have a mirrored effect from the center. Rocaille beads are silver-lined beads. They are sometimes a little bit bigger than other seed beads of the same size. Transparent beads can be clear or colored see-through beads that allow light to pass.

Satin beads appear to have fibers in them.

Metallic beads appear to have a metal look and are coated with any metallic color finish desired. The coatings are fragile and will rub off if handled roughly. They can also be affected by finger oils but are beautiful if handled effectively.

Color-Lined are transparent beads of any color with the hole lined in another color. The color of the outer glass will dominate.

Luster beads are either opaque or transparent and are highly glossy and very shiny.

Pony beads (E beads) are larger than seed beads and sometimes called large seed beads.

Seed beads are sometimes called E-beads. This refers to the shape of the bead. It is not perfectly round (like a druk bead), but rather it is sliced like a loaf of bread gets sliced. Picture the "E" being the shape of the slicer, as it presses down on an elongated tube of glass.

E-beads in the 5/0 to 9/0 size are often referred to as E-beads, while other sizes of seed beads are not. This is probably to differentiate these from perfectly round beads, which are not available in sizes smaller than 2 or 3mm. If a pattern calls for an "E-bead", with no other delineation, it usually wants a size 5/0 or 6/0 seed bead.

Crow beads are twice as big as pony beads. Like the other beads, they come in all styles and colors including wood, brass, silver, gold, acrylic, glass, etc.

Cloisonné beads are enameled metal, and produce a picture or mosaic similar to a stained glass window. These beads come in many colors and shapes. Special "gold", "silver" and "imperial" beads are a little more intricately made.   There are also cloisonné "wiggle" pendants, like fish, turtles and mermaids. These beads look great mixed with brass metal beads, especially the small square brass beads available. For other beads with an oriental design, check out porcelain ceramic beads.

Druk beads are smooth, spherical, pressed glass beads made in the Czech Republic. These beads are made by hand from traditional Bohemian glass. Druk beads are available in many different colors and range in size from 3mm to 18mm. The thread hole is approximately 1mm and smooth for better wear on the thread.   These smooth glass beads come in many fantastic colors and are still made in small quantities by hand, so they will bring unique artisan style to your creations. Use these timeless beads in any kind of project, from intricate beaded necklaces and chunky bracelets, to simple earrings and more.   These versatile beads are a wonderful addition to any look.

Also, many beautiful, patterned pieces can be made with a small Indian bead loom. They are more time consuming and very challenging to use. Many looms are inexpensive to buy.

Under various circumstances, some beads that are dyed or have a coating of some sort, are more prone to fading.

You can use a fixative on your finished beadwork when using the most "fragile" beads, especially when making key chains, pens or other items that receive a lot of handling.

How Glass Beads Are Made - Glass is a mixture of quartz sand and potash or soda, heated with lime. It was invented by the ancient Egyptians and Romans, and later appeared in India. Many cultures made glass. Venetian glass making techniques were regarded as the finest. Glass beads are formed in many different ways. Some of the most prominent today are:

Wound: the bead is formed by the ancient technique of winding molten glass around a metal wire. The beads are then sliced and polished.

Lamp work: a wound glass bead is formed by winding molten glass around copper wire heated over a lamp

Mosaic: mosaic beads are very ornate, and are composed entirely of colorful fused segments of glass cane. Glass cane is a long drawn rod of glass.

Millefiori: these beads have layers of colorful glass fused in cross section and melted onto the surface of a bead. The resulting surface can look like flowers, faces, an abstract pattern, or even a realistic scene.

One example of a glass cross section are two layers of different color glass, rolled up like a jelly roll, and then sliced.

Swarovski Crystal: these are leaded (crystal) glass beads with a very high brilliance. These are named for Daniel Swarovski who was born in Bohemia in 1862, and who invented a machine to cut glass.

Chevron: a very popular bead, first made in the 1400's in Venice. This bead is formed by drawn-out layered glass block sectioned into beads; their ends are cut or ground down to create a zigzag pattern, usually blue with white and red stripes.

Blown: blown glass beads are formed as a craftsman blows into a glass tube that has a small piece of molten glass on the end. The tube is turned over heat until the bead reaches the desired size.

Cloisonné: is an enameling technique in which thin wire partitions (called, cloisons) are filled with enamel. This technique is very old, and was practiced in ancient Byzantium and China. First, delicate strips of copper wire are bent to create a design, then are placed and soldered onto the bead's surface. Next, the spaces are filled with different colored enamels. Finally, the bead is fired and polished several times to produce the desired effect.

Beading Extras

What You Can Make With Beads - Here's some things you can do with beads: Make earrings, necklaces, bracelets, rings, anklets, belts, pins, barrettes, combs, hair bows, book-markers, keychains, magnets for the refrigerator, Christmas ornaments, various types of flowers and mosaics. Also use beads to decorate Christmas stockings and trees (instead of popcorn), decorate clothing (sweat shirts and T-shirts), embroidery, pocketbooks, tote bags and candles. Also use them to decorate those popular, fancy Easter eggs.

Where to Find Beads and Jewelry Findings - Buy beading and jewelry supplies at local Beads and Rocks shops if there are any in your area. Check out jewelry stores, craft, and hobby, fabric and sewing notions shops. Sometimes you can find beads and jewelry findings at some of the local retail outlets such as Walmart. Many mail-order catalogs carry beading supplies. Do a search on the Internet for beads and you will find a treasure trove of places to buy supplies.

When you shop by mail, you never have to leave the house. But since you cannot see what you are ordering, it is best to familiarize yourself with the bead products first. If nothing else, these catalogs will open up a world of ideas and help educate you in what's available for jewelry making. Also, if you are interested in making other crafts, some of these catalogs offer a little bit of everything.

After a while, you will have your favorite places to shop

for the kind of supplies you need and know just where to look for them.

Where to Sell Your Jewelry - You can sell beaded jewelry in many places including: swap meets, church bazaars, wholesale mail order, retail mail order, as gifts for friends, garage sales, yard sales, craft shows, local jewelry shows, music and art festivals, craft parties, gift shops, your own store, specialty (bridal & children's') shops and boutiques, flea markets and consignment. You can use them as fund raisers for scouts, churches and schools. School colors are very popular. Also birthstone colors make nice jewelry accessories.

Make Beaded Jewelry as Gifts - Are you looking for a way to save money on gifts? Wouldn't you like to share a little part of yourself too? Maybe these questions will help you along as you gather some facts about the person that will be receiving your special gift. What are their favorite colors in clothing, etc.? Do they wear earrings and are they clip or pierced? Do they prefer wild styles or are they conservative? Do they like big necklaces or dainty ones? Do they prefer a look that is casual or dressy? Also keep in mind that the person may like something special attached to the jewelry piece (perhaps a coin or a charm). Key chains in various colors make great gifts for the men in your life. Holidays to remember and make beaded gifts.

January 1   New Year's Day
January 17   Martin Luther King, Jr's Birthday
February 14   Valentine's Day
February 21   President's Day

March 17	St. Patrick's Day
April (day varies)	Easter
May 8	Mother's Day
June 14	Flag Day
June 19	Father's Day
July 4	Independence Day
September 5	Labor Day
September 6	Rosh Hashanah
September 15	Yom Kippur
October 10	Columbus Day
October 31	Halloween
November 11	Veterans Day
November 24	Thanksgiving Day
December 25	Christmas Day

Note: Don't forget your family's special holidays and birthdays.

Birthstone jewelry – birthstone colors for each month:
January – Garnet
February - Amethyst
March - Aquamarine
April - Diamond
May - Emerald
June - Pearl
July - Ruby
August - Peridot
September - Blue Sapphire
October - Rose Zircon
November - Topaz
December - Blue Zircon

How to Package Your Jewelry - After all the hard and

loving work you put into making your beaded jewelry pieces and accessories, you think your work is done. However, there's one final thing to be considered and that is how to package them. Here are some inexpensive ways to package finished jewelry pieces and accessories of any kind.

You can buy jewelry cards, or you can make your own. Purchase a 9 x 12 pad of artist sketch vellum. Then cut 3 x 6 squares (6 squares per page) for the long earrings. Sometimes you can use the longer ones for a matched set (short earrings and necklace or bracelet). Cut 3 x 4 squares (9 squares per page) or smaller if desired to use for short earrings, a necklace and/or a bracelet. Punch a tiny hole in the cardboard with a stick pin to hang your earrings and cut notches in the corners to hold your necklaces and/or bracelets.

I couldn't find ready-made jewelry cards large enough to hold my bigger or longer pieces. After some experimentation, I found I could use plain, unlined index cards. They are just the right thickness and come in many lovely colors besides white. I use 4 x 6 cards for my longer earrings. The 3 x 5 cards are great for the smaller pieces.

You might want to color coordinate matched sets. I designed my own lovely letterhead on stationery that matches my jewelry cards. You can also make advertising banners, flyers, bulletins and tri-fold brochures to match and save money from having them printed. If you prefer to have them special made, you can get them anywhere they sell address labels, business cards, etc.

Stick a colored address label at the top of the card that says something like "Designs by Mary" or "Made Just for You," etc. The address labels are an inexpensive way of personalizing your work. You can have up to three or four lines printed on them as needed. You don't have to put your address on them. You can put your phone, e-mail address or anything you want to personalize them and stick them to the index cards.

Those small Styrofoam meat trays that meat and produce comes wrapped in are handy too and come in many colors. You can punch tiny holes in them for your jewelry pieces and cover them in a piece of plastic wrap in the color of your choice. You can add bows or other decorations to your packages.

Some other ways to personalize your jewelry cards are:

Stickers - Stars, hearts, animal shapes, etc.

Splatter paint - Use a spray bottle or splash on with a brush.

Slick or paint writers - Squeeze paint directly from the bottle tip, write name or create unique designs.

Metallic paint pens - These pens contain a metallic paint, great for art or signing your name to your creation.

Photos - Cut slots in your cardboard to slide in the corners of your photo. It's a great idea for Mother's Day.

Markers - These are quick, colorful and readily available. Just be sure to let the ink dry good so it doesn't get on your beaded pieces.

Poster paints - Work great with sponges, just dip the sponge in paint and dab on the card. Create different effects by using more than one color at the same time, or by dabbing the sponge in one color and then another.

You can trim the jewelry cards as needed. You can cut them oval shaped too. Place rings and other things in plastic seal bags without cards if you like. Not every jewelry piece requires a card, but you can organize and prevent tangles this way.

You can purchase the plastic seal bags at your craft shop. They come in different sizes such as 2" x 3", 3" x 4" and 4" x 6". This way, if you have many beaded jewelry pieces and accessories to show, they won't get messed up from fingerprints and dirty hands handling them. They won't get broken as easily either when many people handle them. Trust me; they won't be able to help themselves to a closer look.

You'll find discount packaging and mailing supplies just about anywhere. I purchased index cards and colored stationery at the nearby Walmart. After all your hard work, why not give your beautifully created artwork a special touch in the packaging. Make them sparkle with pride. You will be glad you did.

Getting Started

Materials needed to make basic jewelry:

Scissors - A pair of small, sharp, embroidery scissors with long points for cutting threads close to the beads.

Thread - Use very fine thread (size O or OO) for projects that the thread must go through the beads several times, such as in some styles of earrings. Nymo (nylon) thread is very strong.

Beading Needles - Size 10, 11, 12 or 13. The bigger the size used, the smaller the needle. Size 10 is larger than size 13. A very fine, narrow needle is used for beading because sometimes it is necessary to go through the beads several times. It's a good idea to have an extra needle on hand in case you break one.

Bugle Beads - Use any color and length. Use sizes 3/16", 1/4" and 1/2". They look good with the tiny beads. Also try to mix and match sizes just to see the different looks that can be created, as long as they fit together.

Seed Beads - Use any color, size 10 or 11. The bigger the size used, the smaller the bead. For example, size 11 is a smaller bead than size 10. These sizes are very easy to find.

Ear Wires - Use any type you prefer as long as they have a loop or hole in them so that you can attach them to your earrings.

Other - Use other type of beads, clasps or jewelry findings needed to complete your jewelry pieces.

Remember to keep track of what supplies you used for various projects and where you purchased them in case you want to use them again. This applies to beads, ear wires, etc.

How to Make Simple Necklaces & Bracelets

Cut the thread long enough to go over your head or lay loosely on the wrist leaving extra to tie the knot. You can use heavier thread, stretch elastic, etc. for this because it must go through the beads only once. String the beads of your choice and tie a good knot. They are ready to wear. For shorter pieces, you can also use clasps. They are easy to use by attaching the thread with a good knot at each end. The clasps come in all different shapes, styles and sizes.

If you want to add a charm to the center of your work, string half the beads, add the charm, and then string the other half evenly before making your knot. To make a charm that matches your earrings, make a third earring without an ear wire. Attach it to the center of your necklace or bracelet. They make a charming set.

Make a Ring for Every Finger

You can make charming rings by using stretch elastic. Cut a piece of the elastic longer than needed. String a round base with seed beads. The round shapes are lovely plain or add something special if you like, such as a beaded flower or just another color to set it off in the top of the setting. Tie a sturdy knot and hide it inside the bead.

Color Combinations Ideas

You can use many harmonizing colors such as pastels or autumn tones. Use a rainbow of many colors or the same colors, light & dark. Use three colors such as: red, white and blue.

Other color combinations include: Black and white, yellow, red, lavender, gold, silver or turquoise. You can use white and blue, red, green, pink, purple, lavender or turquoise. Try using gold and green, gold, blue, purple or turquoise. Another good combination is silver and blue, green, pink or turquoise.

If you are a newcomer to beading, start with one or two basic colors. It will be less confusing to you until you learn the basic beading procedures.

Make a list of your favorite colors. You may substitute any other colors of your choice in the jewelry you make and in any pattern you use. You may use all one color too, but using two or more colors will give your jewelry more contrast.

Other Miscellaneous Ideas

Legend of the Indian Dream Catcher - Indians believed that dreams, both good and bad, descended from the night sky. Bad dreams were captured in a web and held there until the rays of the sun evaporated them. Good dreams slipped through the web and passed on to the dreamer.

Fimo is oven-baked polymer clay that is very popular for jewelry making. Fimo colors are more jewelry-oriented (and there are lots of colors available) than other types of clays used for this purpose. The clay is stiffer and requires more kneading before use, but it is especially good for capturing fine details. Finished pieces are strong and durable and you can use glossy and matte lacquers to seal and finish surfaces. You can make and bake your own designs. These pieces are usually glued or fastened to a back or clasp of some type.

Porcupine quills can be used in many styles of jewelry. They should be cleaned before using by dropping them into boiling water for five minutes. Allow them to dry thoroughly on paper towels. The tips are very sharp and will stick you if you are not careful. The quills should be made the same length by trimming off the top and bottom tips. When trimming, hold the point of the quill and cut off the long portion to keep the small sharp points from flying. Use quills that are relatively the same diameter. You can string them through the hollow centers.

Feathers are fun and usually sold by the inch. Sometimes when purchased, they are chain-stitched together in a row at the base and can easily be pulled off undamaged and used as fringes.

Some jewelry styles can be made by sewing the beads

to pieces of leather, chamois, imitation suede that won't fray, lightweight fabric that coordinates with beads or bead cards. Bead cards can be lightweight cardboard such as heavyweight construction paper, manila folders, etc. depending on the stiffness you desire.

Use fine wire to make jewelry pieces. You can also use springy coiled wire that looks like a slinky for bracelets. You can cut off three to five loops and bead together with larger beads. You then bend the ends into small loops with pliers so the beads don't come off.

A rat tail (a rayon tubular braid over a cotton core) is a dressy, sturdy cord that is used as a decorative carrier for special beads, a pendant, etc. You can also use leather strips (the size of shoe laces) for this purpose.

Metal coins can be purchased in silver, gold and a few more colors. Be sure to buy the ones that already have holes punched in them in order to stitch them to your jewelry pieces.

Make Earrings

Follow the instructions below to make earrings (as shown on the cover). This is a diagram of the earring pattern. You will start at Bead 1 (B1).

Use Black opaque #2 (3/16") bugle beads. You will need 53 bugle beads.

Use transparent gold or topaz #11 seed beads. You will need 129 seed beads.

Note: You may substitute any other colors of your choice. You may use all one color, but using two or more colors will give your jewelry more contrast. You can use different color combinations or the same color, such as light green and dark green.

Ear Wire Goes Here

Start Here →
B 1

Bugle Beads
Seed Beads   o

Follow these directions as you refer as needed to the earring illustration guide above. This will be your map. Relax and take your time. Remember, if you make a mistake, you can always pull it out and string the bead again. Good Luck. Now, let's get beading!

Note: These instructions were written using bugle beads for the base. To make a seed bead base instead, follow these instructions and use the correct amount of seed beads in place of bugle beads.

Suggestions:
If you are a beginner, use one or two colors until you can make the basic design. It will be less confusing. Then you can add as many colors as you like later on.

Use 53 black or gold (3/16) bugle beads.
Use 129 transparent amber or topaz (#11) seed beads.

Preparation for Building the Base
Cut approximately 3 yards of thread. Thread your needle. Don't knot the thread.

Step 1
String two bugle beads on thread leaving about a 7 inch tail of thread to the left of the first bugle bead starting at B1 in the diagram.

Step 2
Next, take your needle (N) and thread (T) back through the entry of the first bead. Pull the thread and tighten so that the bugle beads stand side by side in a snug position.

Step 3

Secure this position by simply bringing N & T down through the bugle beads. Gently pull the thread so that the beads stand straight and the thread is taut. Continue in this same way adding one bead at a time until you have completed the bugle bead base. Count and make sure you have the correct amount of bugle heads across when done. Hold your beadwork so that it is flat and does not curl.

Step 4

With the bugle base beaded, secure and strengthen the entire row by weaving back to the beginning bugle bead. When done, N & T must be coming up and out of the first bead with your beginning tail of thread at the bottom of the bead.

STOP and review your work. Is your beads uniform in size? Do they stand straight and even? Is your thread taut and concealed? Does your beadwork lay flat and smooth? If so you are ready to move on to building the upper part.

Step 5

Count across your pattern. Use the correct amount of seed beads to complete the next row located directly above the bugle bead base. String one bead on N & T and pass N & T under the thread that links the first and second bugle beads.

Step 6

Bring N & T back up and through the bead securing the

bead squarely in place above and between bead 1 and bead 2 of the bugle bead base. Simply continue working your way across the row, adding one bead at a time in this way until you have secured the last bead of the row in place.

Step 7
Continue upward. Add and secure the first bead of the next row directly above and between the last two beads of your completed row. Bead across to the end of this new row and continue upward and across, upward and across, until you have beaded your final row of two beads at the top.

STOP and note: There is one less seed bead on a row as you climb to the top of the triangle. If this is done properly, your top is finished. Does it look straight and uniform? If so, now you are ready to go on to making the earring loop.

Step 8
Next you will add the earring loop. This is where you will later attach your earring hook. String your loop beads (two bugle beads). Secure the earring loop in place by bringing N & T back through the top row of the two seed beads. Continue passing N & T through the loop and through the top two beads three or four times in order to make your earring loop stronger.

STOP. Does the top loop look straight? Are the bugle beads used for this step the same size? If so you are ready to work on the lower part.

Step 9

Now you will be returning home to B1. Weave N & T down and through the beads in the body of your beaded triangle to the first bugle bead where you started. N & T must be pointing down and out of that bead (along with the tail you started with). Move the tail over and out of the way so it doesn't become tangled in your work. Now you can string your dangles or fringes.

Step 10

Refer to your pattern so you will string the correct amount of beads necessary for each fringe. String the required beads on the thread and coming out the bottom of the bugle beads. At the end of each fringe, three seed beads serve as an anchor and accent to the strand. String these three beads, returning N & T back through all the beads on the strand except these three accent beads.

STOP. You must adjust these strands as you go. If your fringes appear to hang too short or too long, try taking beads off the strand and using a shorter, smaller or longer, larger bugle or seed bead in their place to make the fringes look uniform according to the pattern.

Step 11

When you have reached the top of the strand, continue passing N & T up and through the first bugle bead, and back down and out of the second bugle bead. Continue stringing this strand and all the other strands in the same way as outlined above, until you have strung your last fringe at the end of the building block.

61

Make sure you have the right amount of fringes when completed.

STOP. In order for the strands of beads to loop and hang gracefully, there must be the right amount of tension or looseness. Take your time to smooth out and adjust them accordingly while still concealing your thread. The fringes move from strand to strand as you gently tug them into place if they are uneven, too tight or too loose. You will learn as you go to do this before making the knots. Also adjust the accent beads. With this completed, you are ready to move on to knotting the thread.

Step 12
Weave N & T up through the beads on the outside edge of your upper beadwork until you are directly above any of the outside beads with threads (which should be every other row). You will form a strong but unnoticeable knot. Tie a double knot here by first going under the outside thread of the bead. Now go back down through that bead with N & T, gently pulling the knot down inside the bead and concealing it. You can hear and feel this little pop. Take the thread through another bead or two toward the middle of you upper bead work to hide it. Cut the thread close to the bead.

Step 13
Rethread your needle on the tail of thread on the first bead of your bugle bead base. Weave up to the outside edge of the earring and knot in the same manner and again concealing the knot and cutting your thread. Dab a little clear nail polish over the top of the bead with the

knot in it to make more sturdy if desired, but this is not necessary.

STOP. Remember, knots must be strong and concealed in a bead.

Step 14
Place a kidney shaped ear wire at the top of the earring by simply pointing the long part of the hook down through the thread atop the loop and then loop around the thread and adjust into position. Or use other type of ear wires if preferred. You can also add the ear wire as you sew the loop at the top, but it can get tangled in the beads as you finish your jewelry piece. This can be done as you become more familiar with beading.

STOP. You have completed your first earring. Use the check list below and see if your work meets the following guidelines. You are now ready to make the other earring to complete a pair.

Final Check List for Finished Beaded Jewelry

Below, you will find a final check list for your finished jewelry pieces. You should use this as your final inspection list so that you have a way of ensuring that your finished jewelry will be perfect. You may want to add a few things to the list as needed. Also, feel free to ignore what doesn't apply. Some companies that buy handcrafted jewelry use a list similar to this one.

Beads are uniform in size.
Color combinations coordinate throughout.
Not too many or not enough beads.
No broken, chipped or irregular beads.
Upper part (earrings) not tilted with loop off center.
Base row not tilted, bugle or seed beads in earrings.
No loose threads showing.
No threads showing under bugle or seed bead base.
No unconcealed knots.
No frayed knots.
No dangles or fringes are crooked and not relaxed.
No dangles or fringes that are too loose.
No curled or bunched beadwork that is too tight.
Hooks are fastened properly.
Both earrings in a pair match same color and length.

Congratulations! You have successfully completed your beautiful, handcrafted jewelry piece.

About the Author

Joann Rohrbach wears many talented and creative hats. She enjoys writing inspiration, poetry, fiction, and non-fiction for all ages. Joann dabbles in digital art, web page design, and music. Along with designing and making beautiful jewelry, she enjoys writing about crafts and hobbies of all kinds. Joann's art appears on her greeting cards, posters, book covers and inside her illustrated books. Other things that she enjoys are cooking, visiting interesting places, reading a good book, spending time with loved ones, collecting angels, and smiles. She brightens up the day for many who know her. More than anything, Joann loves sharing all of her creations with others. Look for more great works by Joann. Visit her website: www.sparklestar.com

About the Book

Beadweaving will show you everything you need to know about beads. You can get started making beautiful jewelry and accessories with all kinds of beads. Sell your creations and make money. Beadweaving is full of helpful information about organizing a work space, managing your time, and packaging your jewelry for sale or just to show off. You will be proud of the beautiful, handcrafted jewelry and accessories that's designed and made by you. Start stringing them along!

More books by Joann Rohrbach
Amazon – amazon.com

It's Halloween! - Halloween is a festive holiday celebrated in many parts of the world. The holiday is sometimes serious but mostly fun, full of mystery and magic. It's Halloween is a book the whole family will enjoy, but especially children. Inside, you will find some interesting facts about Halloween, tips for carving the perfect jack-o'-lantern, trick-or-treating safety tips, and information on how the Heimlich Maneuver saves lives. Have fun making quick and easy recipes, craft projects and more. You may want to leave the lights on as you enjoy reading several short stories for kids of all ages. That is, if you're not too scared!

The Magic of Christmas - The Holiday Season usually starts off with Thanksgiving. Then, the mad rush is on for Christmas before bringing in a New Year. Christmas is a festive holiday celebrated in many parts of the world. The holiday is a time for giving as well as receiving. The Magic of Christmas is a book the whole family will enjoy, but especially children. Inside, you will find some interesting facts about Thanksgiving, Christmas, and the New Year. There's information on how the Heimlich Maneuver saves lives. Take a ride by Model Railroading and learn a little about reindeer. Have fun making quick and easy recipes, craft projects and more. You may want to enjoy reading several short stories for kids of all ages as you sit next to your Christmas tree. There's no place like home for the holidays. May all your holidays be merry and bright!

Love Storm - Love Storm is a collection of love stories for all occasions. It embraces the romantic in all of us. We want to be with that special person, a lifetime partner, who makes us dizzy with happiness. Sometimes we win at love, and other times we lose. They say that all is fair in love and war, but is it? We have to keep believing that our dreams of the perfect lover will come true. Hopefully, love will come to stay.

Mystery Minder - Mystery Minder was written by the "Lady of Mystery" herself. The element of surprise, a nose for news, and a touch of humor, will keep you turning the pages. Are you a sleuth? Can you guess whodunit? Will the villain get their comeuppance? Pull up a chair. You're about to find out!

The Smile Book - The Smile Book is a practical guide about smiles. It was written with a sense of humor, inspirational insights, and many smiles, by "The Smile Lady" herself. Through careful introspection and research, the book offers a view of the smiling universe. There's as many smiles as there are faces. So many smiles and so little time! Have you ever wondered what all those shortcut smileys mean in cyber language? You will find a helpful list included in the book that can be used as a reference guide to interpret and understand the language of emoticons and acronyms.

A Precious Gift - A Precious Gift is a collection of short stories about our most cherished treasures, our children. Many people want children, but can't have them. They often become caregivers to others' children. Raising a child can be a long, tedious, and heartbreaking job. Keeping the faith and believing in a higher power, helps bring love, joy and peace to our lives.

Rain or Shine - Three Books in One - Short Story Collection. Books include Mystery Minder, Love Storm and A Precious Gift.

Celebration of Love - is a beautiful book of love for all seasons. It's full of entertaining articles, stories and poetry about love. A timeless piece of work by the lady of love herself, it makes for warm-hearted reading no matter how young or young-at heart you may be. Burning with emotion, it will move you if read alone or given as a gift. Open the pages, and give yourself the gift of love!

Spirit Star Rising – Spirit Star Series – Volume 1 Melody Lovell expected summer to be humdrum without her friends and parties to enjoy. Having a bothersome, little brother around was enough to ruin anyone's vacation. The one thing she looked forward to was delving deeper into her beloved music. Melody dreamed of meeting her favorite rock singer one day, but was astonished to discover the famous, Willy B. Bold, practically in her back yard, fishing. They shared a common bond and found they made beautiful music together.

Melody experienced adventure, romance, and fun enough to last a lifetime, but not without her share of problems. She learned some important lessons about life, growing up, winning over her rivals, facing the ghosts in her closet, and keeping the evil eye at bay. She often called upon the angels and spirits to help out, but sometimes help came in the most unexpected of ways. She also acquired some family traditions along the way. Making the family's famous recipes and beaded jewelry were a given. Melody also followed in the footsteps of her mother and grandmother and had the gift of psychic intuition and healing. Sometimes, it was a good thing, but not always.

It all happened at her grandparent's quaint, out-of-the-way, lakeside resort in the heart of the Pennsylvania Mountains. Everything was going great until a foolish revelation started a sleuth of fans and reporters on Willy's trail. Since Melody was the cause of all the havoc on Valley View Mountain, she had to do something to help and fast. A little humor, patience, and quick action were necessary to save the day. It didn't hurt to have a spirit star on hand either. Her spirit star, magically transformed into a beautiful love song, became number one on the pop charts. Read it, sing it, live it here!

Spirit Star Falling – Spirit Star Series - Volume 2
Coming Soon.

NOTES

www.ingramcontent.com/pod-product-compliance
Lightning Source LLC
Chambersburg PA
CBHW071238280526
45787CB00002B/983